Developing
Professional Skills:
CIVIL
PROCEDURE

Paula Schaefer
Associate Professor, University of Tennessee College of Law

Series Editor
Colleen Medill

WEST®

MAT # 41231212

© 2013 LEG, Inc. d/b/a West Academic Publishing

610 Opperman Drive
St. Paul, MN 55123
1-800-313-9378

Printed in the United States of America
ISBN: 978-0-314-27953-8

lawyer has the consent of the other lawyer or is authorized by law to do so.

Professional Conduct Rules Link: http://www.vsb.org/pro-guidelines/index.php/rules/transactions-with-persons-other-than-clients/rule4-2/

CHAPTER TEN: Post-Trial Motions

Court: U.S. District Court, District of New Mexico
Local Rules Link: http://www.nmcourt.fed.us/web/DCDOCS/files/LocalCivilRulesAmended 1-1-2012.pdf

Local Rule Stating Court's Professional Conduct Standards:
83.9 Rules of Professional Conduct.
> The Rules of Professional Conduct adopted by the Supreme Court of the State of New Mexico apply except as otherwise provided by local rule or by Court order. *See,* e.g., D.N.M.LR-Civ. 83.4(c). Lawyers appearing in this District must comply with the section for lawyers of "A Creed of Professionalism of the New Mexico Bench and Bar."

Professional Conduct Rule for this Chapter:
N.M. RPC 16-113 Organization as Client

> A. Generally. A lawyer employed or retained by an organization represents the organization acting through its duly authorized constituents

Professional Conduct Rules Link: www.nmonesource.com/nmnxtadmin/NMPublic.aspx

This book is dedicated to
Keith, Henry, and Ben.

Preface

LAW SCHOOLS TODAY aspire to teach professional legal skills.
The current emphasis on skills training is in response to the criticism that
the traditional law school curriculum does not adequately train students
to practice law. The high cost of law school tuition, coupled with the tight
job market for law school graduates in recent years, has intensified the
demand for more skills training in law schools.

Incorporating skills training into doctrinal courses is challenging.
This is particularly true for law school courses that are taught during the
first year of law school. Elaborate simulations can crowd out the coverage
of fundamental legal concepts and doctrines, leaving both the professor
and the students frustrated. The professor feels that there is never enough
time to adequately cover the subject matter. The students feel that there
is never enough time, period.

Developing Professional Skills: Civil Procedure is designed to
provide skills training to law students in a time-efficient manner. Each
chapter in this book focuses on one of the following four core legal skills:

▶ Client Counseling;

▶ Legal Drafting;

▶ Negotiation; and

▶ Advocacy.

     Students are expected to spend about one or two hours outside of the classroom preparing the skills assignment for each chapter. A comprehensive Teacher's Manual contains electronic templates for assignments that can be provided to students. This will allow students to complete and submit the assignments electronically. The Teacher's Manual also gives the professor both guidance and discretion in determining how much classroom discussion time to devote to the material in each chapter. The professor may spend a brief amount of time reviewing the "answer" to the problem presented in the chapter. Or, the professor may expand the discussion to include concepts of professional responsibility and the norms of modern legal practice. Suggestions for incorporating professional responsibility concepts and the norms of legal practice into the classroom discussion are contained in the Teacher's Manual. The Appendix to this book contains the professional conduct rules for the jurisdiction in which the problem is set.

     Developing Professional Skills: Civil Procedure is intended to make the introductory Civil Procedure course fun for the students. The standard classroom routine of reading cases and answering questions generally is not what students envision when they enter law school. As attorneys, students will encounter idiosyncratic, demanding, and occasionally unreasonable clients, constantly evolving new technology, old-fashioned financial and time management constraints, and most of all, interesting problems to solve. Although no book can truly simulate the nuanced tapestry that is modern legal practice, the skills exercises in this book can be used to enhance and enrich the students' educational experience.

I want to thank Professor Colleen Medill at the University of Nebraska College of Law for asking me to be a part of the *Developing Professional Skills* series that she developed for West Academic Publishing. She provided invaluable support at every step of the process. I am fortunate to work at the University of Tennessee College of Law where teaching is valued and a project like this is supported. I am especially grateful to my Tennessee colleagues: Dean Doug Blaze, Professor Judy Cornett, Professor George Kuney, and Professor Alex Long who generously shared their time and expertise. I want to thank my Civil Procedure students who worked through early versions of these problems. Finally, thank you to my tireless research assistants: Anna Gernert, John Rice, Isabel Archuleta, Amy Bergamo, Mitchell Panter, and Rachel Clark.

— Paula Schaefer

Introduction

Developing Professional Skills: Civil Procedure introduces you to skills that differentiate the law student from the experienced legal practitioner. Like any type of skill, acquiring professional legal skills takes time and patience. Most of all, it takes practice. Each chapter in this book provides you with the opportunity to practice a legal skill that you are likely to use again and again after you graduate.

The chapters of this book are organized according to topics that usually are covered in a Civil Procedure course. In Chapter One, you will prepare an outline of the key arguments against a California court's personal jurisdiction over your West Virginia client. In Chapter Two, you will respond to your client's questions regarding subject matter jurisdiction and removal. To complete the problem in Chapter Three you will interview your client and draft a complaint. Then, in Chapter Four you will review a counterclaim and outline key arguments for a motion to dismiss for failure to state a claim upon which relief can be granted.

In Chapter Five, you will learn that you lost the motion to dismiss from Chapter Four. As a result, you will need to draft an answer to the counterclaim. Chapter Six is a negotiation exercise regarding leave to amend a complaint. In Chapter Seven, you will prepare a discovery plan and try your hand at drafting a few discovery requests. Next, Chapter Eight requires attorney teams to negotiate regarding how they will handle inadvertently disclosed document. In Chapter Nine, you will refer to a number of documents to draft a statement of undisputed facts in support of summary judgment. Finally, in Chapter Ten you will write an email to your client describing the post-trial motions you will file.

Client counseling, legal drafting, negotiation and advocacy are the core skills of the legal profession. *Developing Professional Skills: Civil Procedure* provides you with the opportunity to begin to acquire these skills.

Table of Contents

Developing Professional Skills:
CIVIL PROCEDURE

CHAPTER ONE

Personal Jurisdiction
Boots & Shoes Warehouse and the California Landlord

CAITLYN STITES, a partner that you enjoy working with, walks into your office on Friday afternoon. She asks if you have time to talk with her about a new case. You tell her you do, so she takes a seat. You have the following conversation:

> *Caitlyn:* We represent Boots & Shoes Warehouse in a lease dispute with Boots' landlord S.C.A. Property Group L.P. Boots is a West Virginia corporation with its principal place of business here in Charleston. I'm sure you know that Boots sells boots and shoes in stores here in West Virginia. You may not know that they also have stores throughout the Midwest and the South. Boots has been a good client for me through the years.
>
> *You:* I helped you with some motions on a case for Boots last year.
>
> *Caitlyn:* I remember that now. Let me tell you about this case. Boots is leasing property from S.C.A. in Branson, Missouri. They are in the third year of a ten-year lease. For over a year now, they have been arguing about the correct amount of rent due. The rent issue is complicated, but that's not our current problem.

You: OK.

Caitlyn: S.C.A. is based in California, but owns large outlet malls in Missouri and all over the country. Because of the rent dispute, S.C.A. has filed suit against Boots for breach of contract.

You: So we have to defend the lawsuit in Missouri?

Caitlyn: No, not in Missouri—in California.

You: S.C.A. filed suit in California against a West Virginia company for allegedly breaching a lease for property in Missouri?

Caitlyn: That's right—and that's the issue that I need you to research. The lawsuit has been filed in U.S. District Court, Northern District of California. The court has subject matter jurisdiction because the dispute is between citizens of different states and the amount in controversy is more than $75,000. But I think we have a good argument that there is not personal jurisdiction.

You: Is there a forum selection clause in the lease?

Caitlyn: Great question. I brought you a copy of the complaint. The lease is attached and it does not contain a forum selection clause, but it does contain a provision that states that the contract is governed by California law. Paragraph 4 of the complaint states:

> 4. Personal jurisdiction is proper under the California long-arm statute and the U.S. Constitution because Boots & Shoes Warehouse purposefully availed itself of the forum by negotiating, entering into, and performing in California; the dispute arises out of these contacts with California; and this court's exercise of personal jurisdiction is consistent with traditional notions of fair play and substantial justice.

You: Did Boots representatives go to California to negotiate or sign this lease?

Caitlyn: Absolutely not. Obviously, Boots went to Missouri to look at the mall, but the lease was negotiated by phone and e-mail between our folks here in West Virginia and the S.C.A. representatives in their California offices. All of their dealings with each other have been by phone, e-mail, and mail. I understand that the final version of the lease was signed in West Virginia and then mailed to California. All of this is consistent with what has been alleged in the complaint.

You: Have there been any other contacts between Boots and California related to this lease? What do you think S.C.A. means about "performing the lease in California"?

Caitlyn: Boots and S.C.A. have continued to deal with each other since the lease was signed. Again, those contacts have been by phone, e-mail and mail. Boots mails a check to California every month to pay the rent, but no one from Boots has made any trips to California to meet with S.C.A.

You: Does Boots have other connections to California? Does it do any business in California?

Caitlyn: Boots does not accept Internet or catalog orders. It only does business with customers in person in brick and mortar stores—and it has no stores in California. Based on my conversations with the company's representatives, Boots has no contact with California other than its dealings with this California landlord. Boots is not registered to do business in California and was not served with process in California.

You: Do you want me to start working on a motion to dismiss?

Caitlyn: For now, I want you to do some research and put together an outline of the key arguments we can make against personal jurisdiction in California. Be sure to cite authority in your outline. You should also anticipate the arguments that S.C.A. will make and outline how we will attack those arguments.

You: I can do that. When do you need it?

Caitlyn: No rush. Monday morning will be OK. If it looks good, I'll have you draft the motion to dismiss on Monday.

You: Sounds good. I'll get started now.

Points to Consider:

1. *Long-Arm Statute.* California's long-arm statute provides: "A court of this state may exercise jurisdiction on any basis not inconsistent with the Constitution of this state or of the United States." Cal. Civ. Proc. Code § 410.10. Why is the California long-arm statute significant for your research regarding whether a federal court in California has personal jurisdiction over Boots? Would you start with this statute in analyzing whether a state court in California could exercise personal jurisdiction over Boots?

2. *Effective Advocacy.* Even though you are asked to advocate your client's position in this problem, you should not ignore or downplay weaknesses in Boots' position. If you ignore weaknesses, you cannot be prepared to respond to your opponent's argument. As you prepare your outline, consider the arguments you would make on behalf of S.C.A. if you were its attorney. Then consider how Boots can respond to those arguments and incorporate that into your outline.

Outline Your Motion to Dismiss Arguments*

Outline—Attorney Work Product

Motion to Dismiss for Lack of Personal Jurisdiction
S.C.A. Property Group v. Boots & Shoes Warehouse

▶ Key facts that may be important to our analysis:

▶ California Long-Arm Statute
  • Key language:

  • Analysis of Boots & Shoes Warehouse facts under the statute:

▶ Constitutional Analysis
  • Case:
    • Holding:

  • Analysis of Boots & Shoes Warehouse facts under the case:

  • Case:
    • Holding:

  • Analysis of Boots & Shoes Warehouse facts under the case:

* *Your professor may provide you with an electronic version of this template
so that you may complete and submit your assignment electronically.*

• OUTLINE THE KEY ARGUMENTS TO INCLUDE IN A MOTION

- Case:
  - Holding:

  - Analysis of Boots & Shoes Warehouse facts under the case:

- Case:
  - Holding:

  - Analysis of Boots & Shoes Warehouse facts under the case:

▶ Strengths of Boots & Shoes Warehouse's argument:

▶ Weaknesses of Boots & Shoes Warehouse's argument:

CHAPTER TWO

Subject Matter Jurisdiction and Removal
Choose Your Court

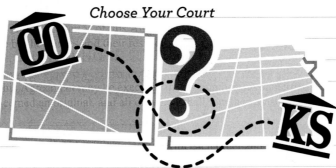

MICHELLE CONNOR was one of your good friends in college, but you have not talked to her for several years. You are surprised to get a phone call from her at your Denver, Colorado law office one afternoon. After making small talk for a few minutes, she says she wants to hire you to be her lawyer.

You: I'm happy to help if I can. What kind of case is it? We do personal injury work at this firm.

Michelle: I know—I saw your billboard on I-70. It's hard to miss. That's why I'm calling. I want you to be "my car accident attorney" like it says on your sign.

You: You were in a car accident? I'm so sorry to hear that.

Michelle: I wasn't driving a car—I was just walking across the street and a guy hit me with his car.

You: Wow, that's awful. Give me the driver's name so I can make sure we aren't representing him in any other case.

Michelle: His name is Ryan Boston. His insurance company is All-Star Insurance. Actually, he is from Kansas and was here in Denver on vacation when he hit me.

You: I just ran a quick check of our clients; we have never had a client named Ryan Boston, and we never represent insurance companies, so we do not have a conflict. Tell me a bit more about your case so I can decide if I will be able to represent you.

99

In your conversation with Michelle, you learn that her medical bills alone exceed $100,000. She gives you some information about the accident and e-mails you a copy of the police report. You tell her you want to take her case. You explain that you will file the case in Colorado, but say that you need to give more thought to whether you will file it in state or federal court.

Later that day, you send her an engagement letter describing your fee arrangement and the terms of your representation. She promptly signs and returns the engagement letter, which she attaches to the following e-mail:

To: You
From: Michelle Connor
Subject: Signed Engagement Letter and My Lawsuit
Attachment: Engagement Letter.pdf

Thanks for agreeing to take my case. I feel better after talking to you. I have signed the engagement letter, and I'm attaching it to this e-mail.

You asked me to send you an e-mail with my address and the other driver's address. Here is that information:

> Me: 5130 Mountain View Way, Denver, Colorado
> Ryan Boston's home address:
> 1109 Castle Road, Wichita, Kansas

I think I understand what you said about filing the lawsuit in Colorado instead of Kansas. That makes sense. Colorado is my home, and I like the idea of having a home court advantage. Plus, Boston caused the accident here in Colorado, so it's fair for him to be sued here.

Here's what I'm confused about. You told me you were thinking about whether we should file the case in federal or state court. Does the plaintiff always have to choose between federal and state court or is there something special about our case? Can you tell me more about state and federal courts or give me a web link so I can read about how they are different? Are there federal and state courts here in Denver or do we have to go to a different city depending on the court we pick?

Does Ryan Boston get any say regarding which court— federal or state—hears this case?

Thanks for explaining this. Sorry to ask so many questions. I appreciate your help on my case.

Thanks,
Michelle

Prepare a brief e-mail in response to Michelle's questions.
Read the following Points to Consider before drafting the e-mail.

Points to Consider:

1. Legal Research. In preparing to answer Michelle's e-mail, research the answers to the following questions:

> **Subject Matter Jurisdiction.** Can the case be filed in a
> Colorado federal court? Colorado state court?
> • Federal court? Legal authority:
> • State court? Legal authority:

> **Removal.** If you file the case in Colorado state court, can the
> defendant remove the case to Federal court?
> • Removal possible? Legal authority:

2. Explaining Your Legal Research to Michelle. Michelle does not care about citations to specific statutes and other legal authority— she is interested in simple answers to her questions. The e-mail should be in your own words. Though she does not specifically request this information, it may be helpful to tell her the name of the specific federal or state court where her case would be filed. She is also concerned about the city where these courts are located. What other information would a non-lawyer client find helpful?

Michelle suggested that you send her some links to information so she can read about the differences between federal and state courts. You should respond to that request, of course, but be selective in choosing the links. Just give her two or three of the most helpful links.

3. Personal Jurisdiction Review. Based on Michelle's e-mail, it sounds like you have decided that the case will be filed in Colorado either in federal or state court. In other words, you think Colorado courts have personal jurisdiction over Ryan Boston. What is the legal basis for this conclusion? Would a court (federal or state) in Kansas also have personal jurisdiction if you sue Ryan Boston there?

Prepare Your E-Mail Reply

From: You

To: Michelle Connor

Subject:

CHAPTER THREE

The Complaint
Fedora Litigation

Memorandum

To: You, Associate

From: Felicia Donna, Partner

Thanks for your great work on the *Harvey* case.
Based on your work on that case, I think you're ready
to take primary responsibility for a new case. It is a
relatively small matter for my client, Nigel Vernon.
I represent Nigel's company on a regular basis. In his
free time, though, Nigel is a Michael Jackson memorabilia collector. He has a large collection of Michael
Jackson memorabilia, including autographed posters
and albums, a statue that once stood in the entryway
of Jackson's Neverland Ranch, and various pieces of
Jackson clothing including one of the white gloves
that Jackson was frequently seen wearing in the 80's.

Nigel has asked us to file a lawsuit on his behalf against
the person who sold him a piece of Michael Jackson
memorabilia that turned out to be a fake. Last summer,
Nigel found a Michael Jackson fedora on the online
auction site eBuy. I have attached a copy of the eBuy
page that shows the final purchase price as $79,000 and
contains the seller's representations about the fedora.
I know that $79,000 sounds like a lot of money, but this

isn't the most expensive piece that Nigel has purchased. Nigel told me he thought it was a reasonable price based on the claim that this is the *one-and-only* fedora that Michael Jackson wore on the Victory Tour in 1984.

Nigel was happy with his purchase until he ran across a story about the groundbreaking for the Smithsonian's National Museum of African American History and Culture ("NMAAHC") in Washington, D.C. He learned that the real Michael Jackson fedora (the one worn in the Victory Tour in 1984 that Nigel believed he had purchased) is currently in the Smithsonian's collection and will be displayed at the NMAAHC museum when it opens in 2015.

Obviously, the fedora that Nigel purchased is not worth $79,000 if the Smithsonian has the real one. Nigel wants to sue the seller, Ashley Taylor. Based on Nigel's information, Taylor lives in Indiana. We will track down an address for her. Because Nigel lives here in Minneapolis, we will plan to file the case in federal court in Minnesota based on diversity jurisdiction. I have already asked another associate to look at the personal jurisdiction and venue issues.

I want you to focus on drafting the rest of the complaint. Under Minnesota law, I think we have a claim for breach of contract and maybe a claim for fraudulent misrepresentation. I want you to interview Nigel, decide whether one or both of these claims are supported by the facts, and draft the complaint. [*Author's Note – in practice you would research other possible causes of action, but for our purposes you should only consider breach of contract and fraud. You may also assume that the elements of those claims are stated correctly below*].

Nigel knows that you will be working on his case. He is going to be in the office talking to me about another case this afternoon, and he says he can stay after and meet with you about the complaint. I think it will be around 3:00.

Before then, put together a rough draft of the complaint so you will be able to ask the right questions and fill in the details based on his knowledge. The elements of a breach of contract claim are relatively straightforward: (1) plaintiff and defendant had a contract, (2) defendant breached the contract, and (3) the plaintiff was thereby damaged. I think we would have no problem alleging facts to support that claim.

My quick research shows that the elements of fraudulent misrepresentation under Minnesota law are: (1) a false representation by defendant of a past or existing material fact susceptible of knowledge; (2) made with knowledge of the falsity of the representation (or made as of the defendant's own knowledge when the defendant did not know if it was true or false); (3) intent to induce plaintiff to act in reliance; (4) causation; and (5) plaintiff suffered pecuniary damage as a result of the reliance.

After you've talked to Nigel and drafted the complaint, you'll want to have Nigel read it carefully to make sure that you have the facts right. I'll look at it too, but I want you to treat this as your case. I think you are ready to handle this with only minimal supervision on my part.

Thanks,
Felicia

Your professor will tell you when and where you will interview Nigel. After your interview, please prepare a draft complaint for Nigel's review.

 Points to Consider

1. *Elements of a Cause of Action.* Partner Felicia Donna does not cite authority when she states the elements of claims for breach of contract and fraudulent misrepresentation. If you want to double check that she has correctly stated the law, what sources will you consult?

2. *Organization of the Complaint.* The numbered paragraphs of a complaint are often separated by headings that help organize the document. The first few numbered paragraphs may follow a heading titled Parties, Jurisdiction, and Venue. The next heading may be General Factual Allegations. The facts in that section tell the story of the case and will help support each cause of action. Thereafter, the following paragraphs are often given headings listing each cause of action as a separate count, such as Count I – Breach of Contract and Count II – Fraudulent Misrepresentation. Each count contains numbered paragraphs detailing the legal elements of the claim and the facts necessary to support those elements.

3. *Client Interview.* Why is it necessary for you to interview Nigel to draft the complaint? Why do you need to send a draft of the complaint to Nigel before you file it with the court? When you e-mail the completed draft complaint to a client for his or her review, it might be tempting to include a very brief note such as: "Please review the attached complaint and let me know if you have any questions or comments." While a note like that may be appropriate for a sophisticated client familiar with a client's role in litigation, a client with less experience in court may want and need more information. What direction and information would be helpful to a client in that situation?

Appendix 3-1

eBuy

MICHAEL JACKSON'S ONE-AND-ONLY 1984 VICTORY TOUR FEDORA

Auction status: Closed 7/21/11
Starting Bid: $10,000
Winning Bid: $79,000 Nigel_101

Seller info:
Ashley_Taylor_29 ☆
Gary, Indiana

78% positive feedback

Accepted forms of payment:
Cashier's Check Only

Description:

THE ONE-AND-ONLY FEDORA MICHAEL JACKSON WORE IN THE 1984 VICTORY TOUR!!!

Own a piece of Michael Jackson history by purchasing this fedora that Jackson wore during the Victory Tour in 1984!!!

Remember that 1984 was the year that Michael won numerous awards for his amazing Thriller album! This fedora was there!!! And if you own the fedora, it will be like you were there, too!!!!!

You have seen this fedora in numerous photographs of Michael and now it can be yours!

Serious bids only!

The fedora will be shipped to you from my hometown – and Michael's – Gary, Indiana! I purchased the fedora in a private auction in 2009, but I no longer feel it is fair for me keep it! I want to share it with the world!!!!

Good luck fans! E-mail me with any questions!!!

Your Client Interview Notes

Notes from Interview with Nigel Vernon

Date:

Attorney-Client Privileged

Attorney Work Product

Your Client Interview Notes

Draft the Complaint*

IN THE UNITED STATES DISTRICT COURT, DISTRICT OF MINNESOTA

NIGEL VERNON, Plaintiff v. ASHLEY TAYLOR 123 ABC Street Gary, Indiana Defendant	)))) Civil Action No. _____))))

Complaint

For his Complaint, plaintiff Nigel Vernon alleges the following:

Parties, Jurisdiction and Venue

1.
2.
3.
4.

General Factual Allegations

5
6.
7.
8.
9.
10.

Your professor may provide you with an electronic version of this template so that you may complete and submit it electronically. You may have a different number of paragraphs in your finished draft.

Count I – Breach of Contract

11.   Plaintiff Nigel Vernon incorporates by references paragraphs 1-10.

12.

13.

14.

15.

Count II – Fraudulent Misrepresentation

16.   Plaintiff Nigel Vernon incorporates by references paragraphs 1-10.

17.

18.

19.

20.

21.

Jury Demand

22.   Pursuant to Rule 38 of the Federal Rules of Civil Procedure, Nigel Vernon demands a jury trial on both of his claims.

WHEREFORE, plaintiff Nigel Vernon seeks judgment in the amount of $79,000, plus punitive damages, costs, and such further relief as the court deems just and proper.

Respectfully Submitted,

By: _____

Attorney's Name

Bar Number

Address

E-mail address

Telephone number

ATTORNEY FOR PLAINTIFF NIGEL VERNON

CHAPTER FOUR

Motion to Dismiss for Failure to State a Claim

Twombly, Iqbal, and Tortious Interference

YOUR CLIENT BOB RADLEY co-owned a greeting card business, Sassy Sentiments, with Charlotte Harris. When they ended their partnership relationship, Harris purchased Radley's interest in the business. Harris is now the sole owner of Sassy Sentiments.

Radley learned that Harris lied about key business matters when they were negotiating her purchase of his share of Sassy Sentiments. On his behalf, you (a law firm associate) and partner Mitchell Davis filed a lawsuit in U.S. District Court, Eastern District of Tennessee against Harris for fraudulent misrepresentation and breach of fiduciary duty. The court has subject matter jurisdiction because the parties are citizens of different states (Tennessee and Georgia) and the amount in controversy exceeds $75,000.

Now, Harris has filed her answer (denying the key allegations of the complaint) and a counterclaim against Bob Radley for tortious interference with business relationship. She apparently believes that Bob is the reason that the company's biggest client is no longer doing business with her.

The counterclaim provides in pertinent part:

IN THE UNITED STATES DISTRICT COURT FOR THE EASTERN DISTRICT OF TENNESSEE IN KNOXVILLE

Bob Radley, PLAINTIFF	))))	
v.	))	Case No. 1:11-00234
Charlotte Harris DEFENDANT	))))	

CHARLOTTE HARRIS'S ANSWER AND COUNTERCLAIM

Charlotte Harris, for her Answer and Counterclaim, alleges the following:

ANSWER AND DEFENSES

omitted

COUNTERCLAIM

I. PARTIES AND JURISDICTION

1. Charlotte Harris ("Harris") is a citizen of the State of Georgia, residing at [address].

2. Bob Radley ("Radley") is a citizen of the State of Tennessee, residing at [address].

3. This Court has supplemental jurisdiction over this Counterclaim pursuant to 28 U.S.C. § 1367(a) because this Counterclaim is so related to the claims stated in the Plaintiff's Complaint that they form part of the same case or controversy under Article III of the United States Constitution.

II. GENERAL FACTUAL ALLEGATIONS

A. THE CREATION OF SASSY SENTIMENTS.

4. On or about April 20, 2008, Radley and Harris entered into a written Partnership Agreement to form Sassy Sentiments.

5. Sassy Sentiments primarily designed, printed, distributed, and sold greeting cards and various invitations in the states of Tennessee and Georgia.

6. The Agreement specified that Radley and Harris were equal partners and that each would be entitled to fifty percent of Sassy Sentiments' profits.

7. Sassy Sentiments regularly provided greeting cards for a number of clients, including Blink! Urban Fashions ("Blink"), a company based in Tennessee. Blink's business with Sassy Sentiments grew steadily, and from January 2009 through September 2010, Blink's order consistently exceeded $3,000 each month.

B. THE DISSOLUTION OF SASSY SENTIMENTS.

8. On or about September 22, 2010, Radley and Harris requested that Sassy Sentiments' attorney begin the process of ending the Partnership.

9. Due to Sassy Sentiments' successful business and continuing business relationships, Harris negotiated to buy Radley's interest in the Partnership so that she could continue operating Sassy Sentiments.

10. On October 17, 2010, Radley and Harris signed a Partnership Termination and Buyout Agreement ("Buyout Agreement"). In the Buyout Agreement, the parties ended their partnership relationship and Harris paid Radley $45,000 to purchase his interest in the business.

11. Also as part of the Buyout Agreement, Radley agreed that he would not compete with Sassy Sentiments in Tennessee and Georgia for a period of two years.

12. Harris thereafter continued operating Sassy Sentiments as a sole proprietorship.

C. RADLEY INTERFERES WITH SASSY SENTIMENTS' BUSINESS.

13. On October 25, 2010, Harris noticed that Blink had not yet placed its regular order for greeting cards from Sassy Sentiments, which Blink usually placed by the tenth of the month.

14. For this reason, Harris contacted Blink to determine whether it was interested in placing its usual order.

15. During this call, Blink placed an order for only $500 instead of its usual order of $3,000.

16. In all subsequent months, Blink has not ordered any cards from Sassy Sentiments.

17. In November 2010, after Blink failed to place an order, Harris contacted Radley to ask if he had been in contact with Blink since the dissolution of the partnership.

18. Radley admitted that he talked to someone at Blink "in September or October 2010," but refused to tell Harris what he said in this conversation.

III. CLAIM FOR RELIEF - TORTIOUS INTERFERENCE WITH BUSINESS RELATIONSHIP

19. Harris incorporates the allegations of paragraphs 1-18 of her counterclaim.

20. At the time of Radley's conduct in September or October 2010, Harris had an ongoing business relationship with Blink through her operation of Sassy Sentiments.

21. Radley was aware that Harris had an ongoing business relationship with Blink through Sassy Sentiments.

22. Radley received $45,000 as part of the Buyout Agreement in consideration for selling his interest to Harris and agreeing not to compete with Harris for two years in Tennessee and Georgia.

23. Radley had contact with Sassy Sentiments' customer, Blink, in September or October 2010.

24. On information and belief, during the conversation, Radley intentionally interfered with Harris's business relationship with Blink.

25. On information and belief, during the conversation, Radley had an improper motive or used an improper means to interfere with Harris's business relationship with Blink.

26. Radley's conduct has caused Harris to suffer both economic loss and damage to her business relationship with Blink.

[The counterclaim concludes with a prayer for relief and counsel's signature].

You discuss the counterclaim with Mitchell (the partner you are working with on the case). He tells you that he has done a little research, hands you a case,[1] and explains that Harris's counterclaim has accurately listed the elements of a claim for tortious interference with business relationship under Tennessee law.

---

1 Mitchell gives you the case *Trau-Med of America, Inc. v. Allstate Ins. Co.*, 71 S.W. 3d 691 (Tenn. 2002), which discusses the elements of a claim for tortious interference with business relationship under Tennessee law.

Mitchell quickly adds, "Stating the elements of the claim is not enough under *Twombly* and *Iqbal* though, so I think we can win a motion to dismiss." Mitchell asks you to do some research and talk to the client.

Your research confirms that a motion to dismiss may work, so you call Bob Radley to discuss. Bob tells you he has read the counterclaim and he is upset by it. He says, "It is true that I talked to Blink's owner. I may have said some bad things about Charlotte's ability to run Sassy Sentiments without me, but I had no way of knowing he would stop doing business with her. That isn't tortious interference with a business relationship, is it?"

You tell him, "It could be, but for now it may not matter. Mitchell and I have done some research and we think we may be able to get the claim thrown out by filing a motion to dismiss." Bob is thrilled. You caution him that the motion may not succeed, and if it does not, you will have to file an answer responding to the allegations of the counterclaim. You also explain what is involved in filing a motion to dismiss. He says that he understands, and he wants you to try to get the counterclaim dismissed.

In preparation for drafting the motion to dismiss under Rule 12(b)(6), create a bullet point outline of your key arguments. Consider which Federal Rules of Civil Procedure are pertinent to your motion to dismiss. You should rely upon *Bell Atlantic Corp. v. Twombly*, 127 S. Ct. 1955 (2007) and *Ashcroft v. Iqbal*, 129 S. Ct. 1937 (2009). You may also want to consider other cases that have applied *Twombley* and *Iqbal*. Note in your outline any difficulties you may face in seeking dismissal.

Points to Consider:

1. Twombly and Iqbal. Does Bob Radley's case highlight a potential shortcoming of *Twombly* and *Iqbal*? Your client admits that he told Blink some "bad things" about Charlotte's ability to run the business. Discovery in the case (from Bob Radley and Blink) may reveal additional details about the conversation that support Harris's cause of action. After hearing all of the evidence, a jury might conclude that Radley's conduct amounts to tortious interference under Tennessee law. Nonetheless, under *Twombly* and *Iqbal*, it is possible that Charlotte Harris's claim will be dismissed before discovery or a trial. That is because Charlotte only suspects tortious interference but does not know (and thus cannot allege with great particularity) what happened behind closed doors. Do you think the U.S. Supreme Court intended that claims like Charlotte Harris's be dismissed?

2. Professional Conduct. Are you engaged in dishonest conduct if you file a motion to dismiss in this case, arguing that Charlotte Harris has failed to state a claim upon which relief can be granted when you know that the facts known to your client may support Charlotte's claim? Is it significant that the motion to dismiss is a legal argument (based on *Twombly and Iqbal*) and not a denial that Radley talked to Blink?

Consider the applicable professional conduct rule, available in the Appendix.

Outline Motion to Dismiss Arguments*

Outline—Attorney Work Product
Motion to Dismiss for Failure to State a Claim
Radley v. Harris

▶ Applicable Federal Rules of Civil Procedure and what they provide:

· Rule 12(b)(6)

· Rule 8

▶ Key points from *Bell Atlantic Corp. v. Twombly*:

▶ Key points from *Ashcroft v. Iqbal*:

** Your professor may provide you with an electronic version of this template
so that you may complete and submit your assignment electronically.*

▶ Additional cases (found in my research) that apply *Twombly* and *Iqbal* that I may want to cite in a motion to dismiss:

▶ Arguments to make that Harris's counterclaim does not satisfy the *Twombly* and *Iqbal* standards:

▶ Possible difficulties we may face in seeking dismissal:

CHAPTER FIVE

The Answer
Tortious Interference Revisited

YOU RECEIVE AN E-MAIL NOTIFICATION that the court has entered an order in the *Radley v. Harris* case (from Chapter Four). You realize that it is probably the court's order ruling on your motion to dismiss Charlotte Harris's counterclaim.

You are excited as you open the document, but quickly become disappointed when you realize that you lost. In its order, the court briefly explains that Harris has pleaded sufficient facts to withstand a motion to dismiss.

The partner working on the case with you, Mitchell Davis, walks into your office. He received the same e-mail from the court. He tells you, "I want you to give the client the bad news and work with him to put the answer together. It shouldn't be too difficult—just deny everything and put in the standard defenses. I have to be out of the office for the rest of the week, but send me a draft by Friday."

In an e-mail, you forward the order to the client, Bob Radley, and explain that Charlotte Harris's counterclaim was not dismissed. You tell him that this means you need to prepare an answer. Bob responds immediately and sets up a call with you for the following day. You have the following conversation with Bob:

You: Bob, I'm sorry about the bad news on the motion to dismiss.

Bob: Me too, but what can you do? So we need to file an answer now? What is that?

You: It's a document that responds to the facts alleged in a complaint—or in our case, the counterclaim. We have to admit or deny each allegation, or tell the court that we don't have enough information to admit or deny.

Bob: OK, that makes sense.

You: Do you have Charlotte's answer and counterclaim in front of you?

Bob: Yes.

You: The first section is her answer to your complaint and the second part is her counterclaim. Let's walk through each allegation in the counterclaim and you can tell me if you agree or disagree with what she says. *[You are referring to the counterclaim found in Chapter Four].*

Bob: OK, I'm ready.

You: I know that paragraphs 1 and 2 are correct because we had that information in the complaint. Paragraph 3 is a legal issue that I can handle. Just so you know, that is correct—the court has jurisdiction.

Bob: OK, then moving on to paragraphs 4 through 6. Everything here regarding the creation of Sassy Sentiments is accurate. You had this same basic information in the complaint.

You: That's right. We also attached the Partnership Agreement as Exhibit A to the complaint. I feel comfortable that those allegations are consistent with what you and I have already discussed and what we alleged in the complaint. What about paragraph 7?

Bob: Blink generally placed an order for around $3,000 each month. I pulled out my records and confirmed that from January 2009 to September 2010, the Blink order always exceeded $3,000. However, that was just Blink's usual monthly order; Sassy Sentiments and Blink did not have any kind of contract for Blink to order that amount each month.

You: OK, that's helpful. Can you e-mail those documents to me? Let's move on to discuss paragraphs 8 through 12. Once again, you and I already talked about these same issues in the complaint—though we didn't focus on the non-compete agreement.

Bob: Right. She has the date right in paragraph 8 and that is what happened. In paragraph 9, I don't know what her motivation was, but we did start negotiating.

You: That is a good point. We will only admit facts that we are certain about. Moving on to 10 and 11, I have the Buyout Agreement. We attached it as Exhibit B to the complaint. I will admit that paragraphs 10 and 11 are correct to the extent that they are consistent with the terms of the Buyout Agreement.

Bob: Yes, that sounds good.

You: What about paragraph 12?

Bob: Well, she is running the business, but I don't know if it's a sole proprietorship.

You: OK, good. I will note that in the answer. Let's move on to paragraphs 13 through 16. Do you know anything about her orders from Blink after the dissolution?

Bob: I don't know anything firsthand about Blink's orders. Charlotte later told me that Blink did not place its regular October order and ended up ordering only $500. I don't know for certain that any of that is true, but that's what she said.

You: OK, what about paragraphs 17 and 18?

Bob: Charlotte did contact me, that's true. She asked if I had talked to anyone at Blink. I didn't refuse to tell her anything, like she alleges in paragraph 18. I told her I had talked to someone at Blink in September or October. And I told her that she should be talking to them, not me! If she was going to run this business without me, I said, she'd need to communicate with the customers. That is something she never had to do when I was her partner. I did all of the marketing for her!

You: That's really helpful, Bob. Thanks. This will allow me to prepare the answer. Later on in this case, Harris's attorney is going to ask us questions in discovery about your conver- sation with Blink. Can you tell me more about that? Who did you talk to?

Bob: It was with Chad Shimley, the owner of Blink.

You: Do you remember that conversation?

Bob: Well, he called me to place his order. I think it was in early October, actually. I told him that Charlotte and I weren't going to be partners anymore and that she was going to be running Sassy Sentiments without me.

You: OK. What did he say?

Bob: Well, Shimley said something nice about how he would miss working with me, and he asked me for Charlotte's contact information.

You: OK. Did you give it to him?

Bob: I told him I wasn't sure how he should contact her, and told him she would probably contact him.

You: All right. Did either of you say anything else?

Bob: Well, I said something that I felt bad about later, but I swear I wasn't trying to cause trouble for Charlotte. I said something like, "I'm not sure she will be able to handle printing and packing all of the orders without me in the business—she has never had to do the hard work on her own." But I never thought he would stop doing business with her.

You: Have you been doing business with Blink?

Bob: Heck no. I wasn't trying to steal her business or anything. I was just talking about how rough things would be for her without me. I didn't mean he should stop doing business with her.

You: OK, I understand. Did you ever talk to him again? Do you know why he stopped ordering from her?

Bob: I haven't talked to him. I have no idea. She really is horrible with the marketing part of the business. He probably stopped ordering because she never asked him to place another order! I really don't know that though; I'm just guessing.

You: Let's finish working on the answer. In paragraph 19 she incorporates the other paragraphs. Then in paragraphs 20 through 26, she adds no new facts. She is just stating the elements of her claim. I'll be able to respond to those with the information we have already discussed. So I think I have everything that I need. I'm going to draft the answer for Mitchell's review and then we'll forward it to you.

Bob: Great. Thanks for your help.

"

Points to Consider

1. Deny Everything. Even though Mitchell told you to "deny everything," you do not think that is the right approach. Confirm your suspicion by reviewing Federal Rules of Civil Procedure 8(b) and 11(b). When you provide Mitchell with the answer that is not a denial of everything, how will you explain your approach?

2. Answer and Defenses. As you draft the answer, be sure to refer to Rule 8 for the proper form of admissions and denials. After responding to each numbered paragraph, include a section titled "Defenses." Refer to Rules 8 and 12, as well as your interview with Bob Radley, as you formulate your defenses.

Draft the Answer*

IN THE UNITED STATES DISTRICT COURT
FOR THE EASTERN DISTRICT OF TENNESSEE
IN KNOXVILLE

Bob Radley,	)	
PLAINTIFF	)	
v.	)	Case No. 1:11-00234
Charlotte Harris	)	
DEFENDANT	)	
	)	

BOB RADLEY'S ANSWER TO
<u>CHARLOTTE HARRIS'S COUNTERCLAIM</u>

Bob Radley, for his Answer to Charlotte Harris's Counterclaim, states the following:

I. PARTIES AND JURISDICTION

1.

2.

3.

* Your professor may provide you with an electronic version of this template so that you may complete and submit your assignment electronically.

II. GENERAL FACTUAL ALLEGATIONS

4.

5.

6.

7.

8.

9.

10.

11.

12.

13.

14.

15.

16.

17.

18.

III. CLAIM FOR RELIEF - TORTIOUS INTERFERENCE
WITH BUSINESS RELATIONSHIP

19.   Radley incorporates his answers to paragraphs 1-18.

20.

21.

22.

23.

24.

25.

26.

BOB RADLEY'S DEFENSES

1.

2.

3.

4.

WHEREFORE, Bob Radley respectfully asks that the Court dismiss Harris's counterclaim with prejudice and enter judgment in Radley favor, award him costs of this action, and grant such further relief that the Court deems just and proper.

Respectfully Submitted,

By: _____

Attorney's Name

Bar Number

Address

E-mail address

Telephone number

ATTORNEY FOR BOB RADLEY

CHAPTER SIX

Amending the Complaint and Relation Back

Mardi Gras Blender Litigation

For the following problem, your professor will assign you to play either the part of John Wheeler, Jr. or Lindsey Vance.

WHILE MAKING HURRICANES for Mardi Gras 2010 (Tuesday, February 16), New Yorker Aaron Journey lost two fingers in a terrible blender accident. Aaron had purchased the blender years ago and no longer had the box or owner's manual. The blender's only identifying mark was the following logo:

It took a couple of years for Aaron to get his life back in order after the accident. So it was not until 2012 that he started thinking about suing the blender manufacturer. He did some research and found two similar "Land" companies that make small household appliances. One was Land Industries, Inc. and the other was Land Corporation. He learned that both corporations are chartered in Delaware with their headquarters in Illinois. Aaron concluded based on his research that Land Industries was the blender's manufacturer.

In fall 2012, Aaron hired John Wheeler, Jr. to be his attorney and showed John his research. John agreed with Aaron's conclusion that Land Industries appeared to be the manufacturer.

On October 10, 2012, John filed a complaint in the U.S. District Court, Southern District of New York against Land Industries seeking over $75,000 in damages. John alleged that Land Industries is liable based on failure to warn and defective product design under New York law. Land Industries was served on October 12, 2012.

On October 31, 2012, Land Industries filed its answer. The pleading contained a general denial of all of the allegations in the complaint. Land Industries' counsel, Lindsey Vance, signed the answer.

In the following months, discovery revealed that Land Industries' CEO, Chairman of the Board, and majority shareholder is Linda Land. Linda signed Defendant's Answers and Objections to Plaintiff's First Interrogatories in which Land Industries denied manufacturing the blender.

Consistent with Defendant's Answers and Objections to Plaintiff's First Interrogatories, Linda Land testified in her deposition on February 18, 2013, that Land Industries does not manufacture blenders. For the first time in the case, John asked about Land Corporation. Linda Land admitted that she is also the CEO, Chairman of the Board, and majority shareholder of Land Corporation. She also admitted that Land Corporation manufactures blenders and confirmed that the "Land" logo that appears on the blender is that of Land Corporation.

The day following the deposition, John called his opposing counsel, Lindsey. They had this conversation:

John: I am planning to amend the complaint to name Land Corporation as the defendant and to dismiss the claim against Land Industries.

Lindsey: I'm happy to hear that you are dismissing the claim against Land Industries but your client is out of luck with Land Corporation. By the way, I represent Land Corporation, too. It is too late for you to sue Land Corporation because the statute of limitations required suit to be filed within three years – which was last week.

John: But my amendment would relate back to the time when the original complaint was filed, making the statute of limitations a non-issue.

Lindsey: I'm not so sure about that. I need to do a bit more research on the issue.

John: If I can convince you that the law favors relation back under these facts, will you consent to the amendment?

Lindsey: I might advise my client to agree to the amendment if the law clearly indicates that relation back of the amendment is appropriate. I'll make time to do the research this week.

John: I'll do the same. My calendar is clear for lunch next Friday. Do you want to meet for lunch and see if we can come to a consensus on the issue?

Lindsey: It looks like Friday is good for me, too. I'll send you an email to work out the details.

Playing your assigned role of John or Lindsey, complete the necessary research and take notes in preparation for Friday's meeting in which John will attempt to convince Lindsey that she (and her client) should consent to the amendment. Lindsey will be open to consenting to the amendment if it appears that a court would give leave to amend and would treat the amendment as relating back to the date the original complaint was filed.

You should rely upon the Federal Rules of Civil Procedure and the amendment and relation back cases in your textbook, unless your professor tells you to complete additional research.

 ## Points to Consider:

1. *Friendly Relationship with Opposing Counsel.* John and Lindsey seem to have a friendly relationship. Do you think it would be difficult to be an advocate for your client if you were on friendly terms with your opposing counsel? Could Lindsey and John's relationship be in their clients' interests?

2. *Negotiation Strategy and Advice to Client.* Lindsey says she might advise her client to consent to the amendment if the law supports relation back. What would Lindsey (and her client) gain by consenting to the amendment? What would they gain by opposing the amendment even if their legal argument appears weak based on Lindsey's research? How should Lindsey talk to her client about these issues? Why should John think about these issues prior to his meeting with Lindsey?

Prepare for the Negotiation*

Attorney Work Product

Attorney Research Notes in Preparation for Negotiation
Aaron Journey v. Land Industries, Inc. (or Land Corporation)

▶ Rules and Case Law

1. Rules and case law governing whether an amendment is allowed:

    a. Rule

    b. Case law

    c. Analysis of our facts

2. Rules and case law governing whether an amended complaint will "relate back" to the original complaint:

    a. Rule

    b. Case law

    c. Analysis of our facts

* *Your professor may provide you with an electronic version of this template so that you may complete and submit your assignment electronically.*

▶ Possible Arguments

1. Should the amendment be permitted?

    a. What will my opponent say?

    b. What is my position?

2. Should the amendment relate back?

    a. What will my opponent say?

    b. What is my position?

CHAPTER SEVEN

Disclosure and Discovery
Tools and Planning

Boots & Shoes Warehouse Redux

YOU FIND THIS E-MAIL in your inbox when you walk into the office at 8:00 a.m. on Monday.

To: You
From: Caitlyn Stites
Subject: Re: Boots & Shoes Warehouse Case

Thanks for your help earlier [in Chapter One] on the Boots & Shoes Warehouse lease dispute with S.C.A. Property Group. Despite our best efforts, it looks like the U.S. District Court, Northern District of California has determined that it has personal jurisdiction. So we are going to have to defend the case there.

As you know, S.C.A. is suing our client, Boots & Shoes Warehouse, for breach of contract. Our defense is that the rent provision in the lease is unenforceable because the Landlord fraudulently changed the rent formula without Boots' knowledge.

Boots' Senior Vice President Teresa Archuleta says that the draft lease included a formula for calculating the rent based on the number of anchor tenants at the mall. The outlet mall contains space for three major retailers—anchor tenants—

who draw lots of customers. It makes sense that a smaller tenant like Boots wants those anchor tenant spaces occupied, because it leads to more traffic and more business.

Teresa says that every draft lease exchanged between the parties contained a base rent that assumed that all three anchor spaces were occupied (as they were when Boots entered the lease) and a downward adjustment formula that allowed a rent reduction when any anchor tenant vacated the mall.

After Boots had been in the space for some time, Teresa learned that two anchor tenants were leaving the Branson mall. She looked to the lease to determine the new amount of rent payable based on the downward adjustment. She saw that the final, signed lease did not contain the formula— it just contained a flat amount of rent due each month.

Teresa pulled up all of the old drafts that she had saved in an e-mail folder and saw that every draft prior to the lease's signing contained the formula with the anchor tenant adjustment. At the time that she signed the lease, she believed she was signing the same document she had seen in her last review with the addition of only two minor changes that she and Boots' outside attorney, Becky Mills, had requested.

Teresa believes that the last minute change was intentionally made to defraud Boots. Teresa still has an e-mail from the landlord stating, "We made the last two changes you requested. Please sign and mail your signed copy back to us." Teresa insists that the change was no accident and must have been inserted by one of three people: John Brice (the landlord's representative who signed the lease), Hunter Rush (the landlord's in-house attorney), or another attorney (who probably worked at an outside law firm) whose name Teresa cannot remember. Even though all of the prior versions of the draft lease were forwarded in Word format, the final lease was sent as a PDF.

After the anchor tenants left, Boots decided to pay the rent amount based on the formula in the last draft lease. Of course, S.C.A. was furious and spent more than a year exchanging letters with Boots debating the correct rent amount. With the rent discrepancy and substantial late fees it claims to be entitled to, S.C.A.'s lawsuit seeks over $75,000 in damages.

So those are the facts. At this point, we need to start planning for discovery. Our local counsel in California will help make sure we are following all of the local rules, but we are going to take the lead here in West Virginia. I am going to work with Teresa, who is our main contact at Boots for this case, to prepare our initial disclosures and to get ready for the upcoming Rule 26(f) conference. I have already issued a written litigation hold, and I have met with three key players at Boots and the company's IT manager to make sure we are preserving all potentially discoverable information on our side.

I need you to take the lead on making a plan for discovery of information in S.C.A. Property Group's possession. I have been brainstorming about the categories of information we need to request from them; they are listed below. I want you to make a plan for the most effective way to get that information: through initial disclosures from the Landlord, interrogatories, requests for production of documents, depositions, or requests for admissions. If you think a request for production, interrogatory, or request for admission is the way to go, please draft the request. As you are planning and drafting, you should think of other categories of documents and information that we need and make a plan to obtain it.

We need to uncover the following facts:

- Names of S.C.A. Property Group's attorneys and other agents involved in negotiating and drafting the lease.

• Evidence that someone on the S.C.A. side made the change to the lease, without telling Boots, intending that Boots would not notice until it was too late.

— I think we should get all drafts of the lease in native format with metadata. It appears that the draft leases that S.C.A. e-mailed to Teresa during negotiations were all scrubbed of metadata and the final version is a PDF. Getting the native files with metadata may allow us to determine who made the change to the lease.

— Do you have other ideas about how we can get S.C.A. to admit to its fraud? What questions (in depositions or interrogatories) should we ask to get this information? Are there other documents we should request? Let me know your thoughts and your plan for getting this information.

• Leases for other tenants in the same Branson mall. Maybe S.C.A. has done this before!

Remember, we need to be efficient in getting this discovery through the most cost-effective means. When you are done with your discovery plan, e-mail it to me. I will look it over and provide you with any input I have.

Points to Consider:

1. Do You Want Broad Discovery? Federal Rule of Civil Procedure 26(b) provides for broad discovery: generally, a party is entitled to discover any non-privileged matter relevant to a claim or defense. The requested information need not be admissible but only "reasonably calculated to lead to the discovery of admissible evidence." Even though your client may be entitled to broad discovery under this rule, what are the reasons that you may want to make more narrow and focused discovery requests?

2. *Proper Use of Examples, Forms, and Templates.* Most junior attorneys who are asked to do something for the first time want to see an example, form, or template. While looking at an example can be a helpful starting point, remember that discovery's primary purpose is to discover facts of the case you are working on. Tailoring your discovery requests to the issues in your case is a more efficient way to conduct discovery than borrowing broad interrogatories and requests for production from some other case. This same reasoning also applies to objecting to an opponent's discovery requests. While it may be tempting to use someone else's broad, boilerplate objections, discovery works best when attorneys provide precise objections and explain what information, if any, is being withheld on the basis of those objections.

Prepare a Discovery Plan*

Discovery Plan - Attorney Work Product
S.C.A. Property Group v. Boots & Shoes Warehouse

▶ Names of S.C.A. Property Group's attorneys and other agents involved in negotiating and drafting the Lease.

• Best discovery tool to obtain this information (initial disclosures, interrogatories, request for production, etc.):

• Draft discovery request:

▶ Evidence that someone on the S.C.A. side made the change to the lease, without telling Boots, intending that Boots would not notice until it was too late.

• Information needed:
  1. Drafts of the lease in native format with metadata.

  2.

  3.

  4.

  5.

* Your professor may provide you with an electronic version of this template so that you may complete and submit your assignment electronically.

• Discovery tool I will use for each:

    1.

    2.

    3.

    4.

    5.

• Draft a discovery request for each:

    1.

    2.

    3.

    4.

    5.

▶ Leases for other tenants in the same Branson mall.

    • Discovery tool:

    • Draft a discovery request:

▶ Other ideas for information needed in discovery (for each idea, list the tool you will use to get the information and draft your discovery request).

    •

    •

    •

    •

    •

CHAPTER EIGHT

Inadvertent Disclosure
Teresa, Terrence, and the
Hazards of E-mail Autocomplete

For the following problem, your professor will assign you to
play either the part of Anna Garret or Teresa McDonald.

ANNA GARRET AND TERESA MCDONALD are attorneys representing opposite sides in litigation pending in the U.S. District Court, Middle District of Florida.

Anna is one of the attorneys at the firm Mills & Fleming, LLP, handling the defense of Better Pharmaceuticals, Inc. Anna is the most junior attorney on the case; Maggie Crabapple is the lead attorney.

Teresa is the junior lawyer on the other side of the case representing plaintiff Lora Lancaster. Every attorney in Teresa's small firm, Baker & Scarborough, is involved in some aspect of the case. Rick Scarborough is the lead attorney on their side and the managing partner of the Baker & Scarborough firm.

As the junior attorneys on the case, Anna and Teresa regularly correspond about discovery issues. They have a respectful, professional relationship but do not know one another personally. They practice in different cities in Florida.

In the lawsuit based on state law claims, plaintiff Lora claims that she was not warned that BPI's top-selling high blood pressure drug, Lethora, causes rapid weight gain, rapid hair growth (all over the patient's body), and memory loss. Further, the medication is highly addictive, so even when Lora recognized the medication's adverse side effects, it took her almost a year before she could break her addiction and stop taking the drug. Lora is now suing BPI to recover for her injuries.

Anna sent the following e-mail to Teresa by accident. She intended to send the message to Terrence Hardy, the assistant general counsel at BPI who is Anna's primary contact for the case. Anna's e-mail program has an autocomplete function that suggests names as the user types. So when Anna typed "Ter" one option provided was Teresa McDonald and another was Terrence Hardy. Apparently, Anna selected the wrong option and sent this e-mail to Teresa.

To:	Teresa McDonald
From:	Anna Garret
Subject:	Lancaster Case
Attachment:	Memo re Lancaster Claims, Defenses and Settlement Demand.docx

Hi Terrence:

Maggie is traveling today, so she asked me to forward a document for your review. As you requested, we put together a memo analyzing the strength of plaintiff's claims and BPI's defenses in the Lancaster case. The memo contains a summary and analysis of the key legal and factual issues (based on discovery completed so far and our internal investigation) for each claim. The memo concludes with our suggestions regarding a response to the plaintiff's most recent settlement demand.

Please contact me if you have any questions.
— Anna

At the Law Offices of Baker & Scarborough

Teresa read the entire e-mail message as soon as she received it, but she did not open the attachment. When she finished reading the e-mail, Teresa walked to Rick Scarborough's office to ask him what to do. They had the following conversation:

> *Teresa:* I just received an e-mail from BPI's attorneys in the Lancaster case. The e-mail was obviously intended for their client and not for me. There is an attachment that analyzes the strengths and weaknesses of their case and discusses settlement. I haven't read it yet. Do you want me to forward the e-mail to you?
>
> *Rick:* No, I don't want to see it. I want you to do some research about what we are required to do when we receive an inadvertent disclosure.
>
> *Teresa*: OK, I'll do some quick research. Where should I start?
>
> *Rick*: Be sure to research the professional conduct rules adopted in the U.S. District Court, Middle District of Florida. There is a rule about inadvertent disclosure. Then, look at the Federal Rules of Civil Procedure. I seem to remember that Rule 26 says something about returning documents produced by accident by another party. There is also a rule of evidence that deals with inadvertent disclosure I think it's Federal Rule of Evidence Rule 502. You should look at that, too.
>
> *Teresa:* I think the court's scheduling order says something about inadvertent disclosure, too.

Rick: Good point. I should have thought of that. Most people call it a clawback order. I remember we discussed having one in our 26(f) conference.

Teresa: Is that all?

Rick: Even if we have to give the document back in the short term, we may have an argument that the privilege has been waived by the disclosure. If this attachment is something we would like to use in the case, it might be worth it to make a waiver argument. Think about that as you do your research. Federal Rule of Evidence 502 discusses waiver, but you may need to do a little case law research too.

At the Law Offices of Mills & Fleming, LLP

Anna received a call from Maggie Crabapple later in the day:

Maggie: I just talked to Terrence. He says that he has not heard anything from us on the settlement issue. I thought you were going to send that memo to him this morning.

Anna: I did. Let me check my sent folder. I'll be able to tell you what time it was sent. Maybe it went to his spam folder. Let me see. . . . oh, no! I sent the memo, but I accidentally sent it to Teresa McDonald, opposing counsel on the Lancaster case. I am so sorry. I have no idea how this happened.

Maggie: OK, we need to move on this fast. You'll need to talk to Teresa to find out if she has read the e-mail and attachment or shared the information with anyone. You will also need to ask her to delete the e-mail and attachment.

Anna: I will do that right now.

Maggie: Anna, it will help if you can cite some authority when you talk to her. I think the professional conduct rules and the Federal Rules of Civil Procedure cover this issue. See what you can find. Remember, the professional conduct rules are in the local rules for the Middle District of Florida, where the case is pending. I'm pretty sure the Middle District follows Florida's rules of professional conduct.

Anna: OK, I'll look. What about that clawback agreement you had me draft for the 26(f) report? That deals with inadvertent disclosure.

Maggie: You're right. The court incorporated that clawback agreement into the scheduling order in this case, making it a "clawback order." Maybe that will give us an answer.

Anna: I am so sorry. I will try to do some research in the next hour, and then give you a call to let you know what I find before I call Teresa.

Maggie: And remember, getting the document back in the short term may not be the end of the issue. Even if Teresa deletes the e-mail, she may still go to the court and ask for a ruling that we waived privilege and that we have to return the document to her. So as you research, be sure to consider the strength of their possible argument that we waived privilege by the disclosure. Waiver is covered by Federal Rule of Evidence 502, unless that issue is addressed by the clawback order.

"

Both junior attorneys found the following clawback provision in the court's scheduling order:

> *If a party inadvertently discloses a privileged or work product protected document in this case, privilege or work product protection is not waived by the disclosure if the sending attorney used reasonable precautions to prevent the disclosure and promptly requested the document's return.*

Both Teresa and Anna spent approximately one hour researching various inadvertent disclosure authorities mentioned by the senior attorneys in their respective firms. Each prepared a bullet-point outline of key issues to discuss with each other. *Playing your assigned role, you should complete the research and outline.*

Both Teresa and Anna talked to their supervising attorneys about their research. *You should assume that your supervising attorney agreed with your approach to handling the issue.*

Having learned her lesson about the perils of e-mail, Anna decided to call rather than e-mail Teresa. They had the following conversation:

Anna: Hi Teresa. Earlier today, I inadvertently sent you an e-mail that was intended for my client.

Teresa: I'm glad you called. I was planning to call you to let you know that I received the e-mail. I haven't opened the attachment yet because I wanted a chance to do some research and talk to you first.

Anna: I did some research too. Let's talk about what you're planning to do with the e-mail and attachment. I hope I can convince you that you should delete it.

Playing your assigned role, you will meet with your opposing counsel to negotiate a possible resolution of two issues:

1. In the short term, should Teresa delete or sequester the e-mail and attachment?

2. In the long term, should Teresa seek a ruling that privilege was waived by the disclosure (which would clear the way for Teresa to keep the document and make use of it)?

Both attorneys understand that the outcome of their negotiation will be reported to their supervising attorneys and clients who may have additional input on the matter.

 Points to Consider:

1. Protecting the Content of the Inadvertently Disclosed Privileged Document Pending a Waiver Ruling. While professional conduct rules and civil procedure rules cannot resolve the issue of whether an inadvertent disclosure results in privilege waiver, these rules can give recipients of an inadvertent disclosure ("receiving lawyers") direction about what measures they must take to protect the content of the disclosed document pending a waiver ruling. As you research these rules, consider what event triggers a receiving lawyer's obligation under each rule and what steps the receiving lawyer must take after the triggering event.

2. *Privilege Waiver.* If parties do not agree on the issue, courts get the final say about what happens to an inadvertently disclosed document. Either attorney can seek a ruling on the issue of whether privilege was waived by the disclosure. Federal Rule of Evidence 502(b) states the test for privilege waiver, but because of the subjective nature of that test, it is difficult to know how a court will resolve the issue. Does this lingering possibility of waiver make a receiving attorney more or less likely to seek a waiver ruling when an intriguing privileged document is inadvertently disclosed?

3. *Clawback Agreements.* Now that you know something about professional conduct rules, civil procedure rules, and evidence rules and their role in the inadvertent disclosure puzzle, you are ready to think about clawback agreements. These party agreements (that are often incorporated into court orders) can supplant the standards found in all of the foregoing rules. Why would you enter a clawback agreement instead of relying on the rules that are otherwise in place? As you think about the goals of a clawback agreement or order, consider whether Anna and Teresa's clawback accomplishes any of those goals.

4. *Non-Legal Considerations.* Beyond the law, what other issues should the attorneys and their clients consider as they discuss how they will resolve the inadvertent disclosure?

Inadvertent Disclosure Research and Plan*

Attorney Work Product
Lancaster v. Better Pharmaceuticals, Inc.

▶ Professional Conduct Rules in the Middle District of Florida
(available in the Appendix):
  - Rule:
  - Application to this case:

▶ Federal Rules of Civil Procedure:
  - Rule:
  - Application to this case:

▶ Federal Rules of Evidence:
  - Rule:
  - Application to this case:

* Your professor may provide you with an electronic version of this template so that you may complete and submit your assignment electronically.

▶ Case Law:

    • Holding:

    • Application to this case:

▶ Clawback Order in this Case

    • Key language:

    • Does it override the foregoing authorities?
    How will it be applied in this case?

▶ Plan for your negotiation with opposing counsel:

1. In the short term, should Teresa delete or sequester the e-mail and attachment?

• Legal authority and analysis to support your position.

• Non-legal considerations.

• How do you think your opponent will resolve this issue?

• How will you respond?

2. In the long term, should Teresa seek a ruling that privilege was waived by the disclosure? If so, will she prevail on the motion?

• Legal authority and analysis to support your position.

• Non-legal considerations.

• How do you think your opponent will resolve this issue?

• How will you respond?

CHAPTER NINE

Summary Judgment
Long-Lost Siblings and the Life Insurance Policy

YOUR CLIENT, Amy Berger, is involved in litigation with her half-siblings about the proceeds of a life insurance policy.

Amy grew up not knowing anything about her biological father other than her mom Violet Berger's explanation that "Bob was my college boyfriend and we broke up long before you were born." When she was sixteen and preparing to get her driver's license, Amy saw her father's full name on her birth certificate. Because it was a rather common name, Robert Stephenson, there was no easy way to find him without her mother's help. Amy was not interested, so she did not ask.

In 2007, when Amy was twenty-five and interested in meeting Bob, she asked Violet for more details about him. With information about Bob's hometown and family, Amy was able to track him down in Virginia. Amy was living in Maine (as she had her entire life), so her first contact with Bob was by phone.

Bob was shocked to get Amy's phone call. He had no idea that he had a daughter with Violet, but he did not doubt that it was true. He confirmed Violet's story—that as college students, the two had lived together but, after a bad break up, they never spoke again.

Initially, Amy and Bob got to know each other by talking on the phone and exchanging e-mail. They exchanged photos and both agreed they shared a number of physical features, including the same bright red hair. Neither felt it was necessary to get a DNA test to confirm their relationship; both believed that Bob was Amy's father.

Bob had been divorced for a number of years when Amy contacted him. He never remarried and remained close to his two children from his marriage—Stan and Stu Stephenson. The boys were nineteen and seventeen in 2007 (the year when Amy contacted Bob). Bob paid for Amy to visit him and his extended family in Virginia in 2008. Bob introduced Amy to Stan and Stu, explaining that Amy was his daughter from a relationship he had when he was in college. The boys were friendly to Amy, but none of the siblings made an effort to stay in touch in the years that followed.

Amy and Bob stayed in touch, though, and developed a good relationship. In fall 2010, Amy was devastated by Bob's news that he had been diagnosed with cancer and that his prognosis was not good. In an e-mail dated October 30, 2010, Bob told Amy that he had named her as a beneficiary on his life insurance policy. He e-mailed Amy a document titled Endorsement of Change of Beneficiary showing that she, Stan, and Stu would each receive 1/3 of the proceeds from a $1 million life insurance policy.

Bob died in 2011. Amy made a claim with the life insurance company, Virginia Life Insurance Company, but the claim was not paid because Stan and Stu claimed that the change of beneficiary form was invalid.

Stan and Stu made that claim in a letter written on their behalf by their attorney, Crystal Keith. She provided Virginia Life Insurance Company with Stan and Stu's parents' Divorce Decree, which incorporated a Settlement Agreement. The Settlement Agreement states in pertinent part:

22. Life Insurance. In 1990, Husband and Wife each obtained a thirty-year level term life insurance policy (insurance in the amount of $1 million) with Virginia Life Insurance Company. Husband's policy number is 1,970,108; Wife's policy number is 1,970,010. Husband's annual premium for the thirty-year level term is $695; Wife's annual premium for the thirty-year level term is $640. We both agree that we will maintain these policies for the full thirty-year level term solely for the benefit of our children, including any children born or adopted to either of us after our divorce. We agree that we will not change the beneficiary to any person other than our own children and that each such child named as a beneficiary will receive an equal share of the proceeds. Upon signing this Agreement, we will submit Change of Beneficiary forms to Virginia Life Insurance to name as primary beneficiary: Stanley Ralph Stephenson (50%) and Stuart Arthur Stephenson (50%).

In her letter to Virginia Life Insurance Company, Crystal Keith argued that this language prohibited Robert Stephenson from naming Amy Berger as a beneficiary because (1) even if Amy is Robert's child (something that has never been established), she was not one of "our children" contemplated by the Settlement Agreement; and (2) Amy was not "children born or adopted to either of us after our divorce."

In 2012, Virginia Life Insurance filed an interpleader action in U.S. District Court, Eastern District of Virginia, naming Amy, Stan, and Stu as defendants. Amy continues to reside in Maine, while Stan now lives in Florida and Stu lives in Georgia. You represent Amy in that case; Crystal Keith represents Stan and Stu.

In your view, summary judgment is appropriate now that discovery is complete. You believe there is no genuine dispute regarding the material facts. No one disputes the genuineness of any of the life insurance documents or the Divorce Decree and Settlement Agreement. Further, all of the evidence is consistent with Amy being Bob's daughter even though Stan and Stu have questioned that fact throughout the case.

You believe that the only question that remains is a legal one— does the language of the Settlement Agreement permit Bob to add a child (whom he did not know about in 2000) as a beneficiary? You think that the question will be resolved by legal rules of contract construction under Virginia law and that the law supports the validity of Amy receiving an equal share of the life insurance proceeds.

Be sure to read Federal Rule of Civil Procedure 56 and local rules for the U.S. District Court, Eastern District of Virginia regarding summary judgment. Then, prepare the Statement of Undisputed Facts to support your motion for summary judgment. For each undisputed fact, cite the evidence that you will use to support the fact and mark that evidence as an exhibit. You will find some documents in the appendix to this chapter that you may want to use.

 Points to Consider

1. *Preparing the Statement of Undisputed Facts.* The Statement of Undisputed Facts should be presented as a series of numbered paragraphs with each paragraph containing a single fact supported by one or more exhibits (such as Amy's birth certificate, which might be marked "Exhibit A."). Affidavits or declarations of witnesses often accompany a Statement of Undisputed Facts and are also marked as exhibits.[1]

---

1 An affidavit is a witness's written statement that is sworn to under oath before an officer authorized to administer oaths, such as a notary; a declaration is a witness's unsworn written statement. Both declarations and affidavits are permitted under Federal Rule of Civil Procedure 56(c)(4) and are usually formatted as a series of numbered paragraphs.

You might consider drafting an affidavit or declaration for Amy Berger in this case. In Amy's affidavit, she would state facts known to her that would be admissible in evidence if she were to testify at trial. *See* Fed. R. Civ. P. 56(c)(4).

2. Seeing the Big Picture of Summary Judgment. Your Statement of Undisputed Facts will be part of your Memorandum in Support of Summary Judgment. In your argument supporting summary judgment, you would cite case law to support your contract interpretation argument (in short, that the term "children" includes Amy) and argue that given the undisputed facts, your client is entitled to judgment as a matter of law.

3. Anticipating the Stephenson Opposition. The Stephenson brothers might oppose your motion for summary judgment by citing materials that demonstrate a dispute about the material facts, by showing that your materials do not establish that the material facts are undisputed, by objecting that your evidence cannot be presented in an admissible form, or by arguing that more time is needed for discovery. *See* Fed. R. Civ. P. 56(c)(1), (2), and (d). After you have drafted your Statement of Undisputed Facts, consider which of these methods of attack concerns you the most. Alternatively, the Stephenson brothers might file a cross-motion for summary judgment agreeing that the material facts are undisputed but arguing that the law supports their interpretation of the contract ("children" does not include Amy).

Draft the Statement of the Undisputed Facts*

IN THE UNITED STATES DISTRICT COURT
FOR THE EASTERN DISTRICT OF VIRGINIA

VIRGINIA LIFE)	
INSURANCE COMPANY,)	
Plaintiff)	
v.)	No. 12-cv-1799829
)	
AMY BERGER,)	
STANLEY STEPHENSON,)	
AND STUART STEPHENSON,)	
Defendants)	
)	

MEMORANDUM IN SUPPORT OF AMY BERGER'S
MOTION FOR SUMMARY JUDGMENT

Pursuant to Rule 56 of the Federal Rules of Civil Procedure, defendant Amy Berger submits this Memorandum in Support of her Motion for Summary Judgment.

I. Introduction

[omitted]

II. Statement of Undisputed Facts

1.

2.

3.

4.

5.

Your professor may provide you with an electronic version of this template so that you may complete and submit your assignment electronically. You may have a different number of undisputed facts in your completed document

III. Argument

[omitted]

For the foregoing reasons, Amy Berger respectfully asks that the court enter summary judgment in her favor.

Respectfully Submitted,

By: _____
Attorney's Name
Bar Number
Address
E-mail address
Telephone number
ATTORNEY FOR AMY BERGER

Appendix 9-1

Settlement Agreement in Contemplation of Divorce

On this 31st day of May 1996, Robert A. Stephenson and Carolyn G. Stephenson enter into this Settlement Agreement in Contemplation of Divorce and agree as follows:

A. Husband and Wife were married on July 1, 1986 and they had two children: Stanley Ralph (DOB 03/04/88) Stuart Arthur (DOB 02/27/90); and

B. Irreconcilable differences have caused Husband and Wife to separate and seek a divorce; and

C. Husband and Wife wish to divide their property and agree upon their obligations to each other and to their children; and

D. Husband and Wife will request that the Court incorporate the terms of this Agreement into a final decree of divorce.

Based upon the foregoing agreed upon recitals, the parties enter this Settlement Agreement in Contemplation of Divorce:

[paragraphs 1-3]

4. Governing Law. This Agreement shall be construed and governed in accordance with the laws of the Commonwealth of Virginia.

[paragraphs 5-22]

22. Life Insurance. In 1990, Husband and Wife each obtained a thirty-year level term life insurance policy (insurance in the amount of $1 million) with Virginia Life Insurance. Husband's policy number is 1,970,108; Wife's policy number is 1,970,010. Husband's annual premium for the thirty-year level term is $695; Wife's annual premium for the thirty-year level term is $640. We both agree that we will maintain these policies for the full thirty-year level term solely for the benefit of our children, including any children born or adopted to either of us after our divorce. We agree that we will not change the beneficiary to any person other than our own children and that each such child named as a beneficiary will receive an equal share of the proceeds. Upon signing this Agreement, we will submit Change of Beneficiary forms to Virginia Life Insurance to name as primary beneficiary: Stanley Ralph Stephenson (50%) and Stuart Arthur Stephenson (50%).

[paragraphs 23-30]

[Notarized signatures of both parties]

Appendix 9-2

IN THE CIRCUIT COURT FOR ARLINGTON COUNTY, VIRGINIA

Carolyn G. Stephenson
Plaintiff

v.   CL No. 1996- 1 1673

Robert A. Stephenson
Defendant

Final Decree of Divorce

Having considered the testimony and evidence presented by the parties and counsel, the court makes the following findings:

1. The Court has jurisdiction over the subject matter and the parties who have both been residents of this state since their marriage in this state on July 1, 1986.

2. Two children were born to the couple during their marriage: Stanley Ralph Stephenson, born March 4, 1988, and Stuart Arthur Stephenson, born February 27, 1990.

3. The husband (advised by his own counsel) and the wife (advised by her own counsel) have voluntarily entered into a fair and equitable Settlement Agreement in Contemplation of Divorce dated August 31, 1996 (attached and incorporated herein by reference).

4. The marriage is irretrievably broken.

THEREFORE, it is ORDERED, ADJUDGED AND DECREED:

The marriage between the parties is dissolved.

The May 31, 1996 Settlement Agreement in Contemplation of Divorce is approved and incorporated in this Decree of Dissolution by reference. The parties are ordered to comply with its terms and the court reserves jurisdiction to compel either party to perform the terms of the Agreement.

Signed this 1st day of November 1996.

Jamey Walters

Jamey Walters, Judge

Appendix 9-3

Virginia Life Insurance Company

ENDORSEMENT OF CHANGE OF BENEFICIARY

Insured: Robert Stephenson

Policy Number: 1,970,108

As requested by you on August 31, 1996, your beneficiary designation has been amended to provide for the following. Please retain this Endorsement with your Policy.

Primary Beneficiary: Stanley Ralph Stephenson, son (50%); and Stuart Arthur Stephenson, son (50%).

Contingent Beneficiary: Estate of Robert Stephenson.

Appendix 9-4

Virginia Life Insurance Company

ENDORSEMENT OF CHANGE OF BENEFICIARY

Insured: Robert Stephenson

Policy Number: 1,970,108

As requested by you on October 7, 2010, your beneficiary designation has been amended to provide for the following. Please retain this Endorsement with your Policy.

Primary Beneficiary: Amy Berger, daughter (33.3%); Stanley Ralph Stephenson, son (33.3%); and Stuart Arthur Stephenson, son (33.3%).

Contingent Beneficiary: Estate of Robert Stephenson.

Appendix 9-5

To: Amy Berger
From: Bob Stephenson
Subject: Insurance
Attachments: endorsement.pdf

Hi Amy,

I know this is hard for us to talk about, but I am trying to make some preparations for what will happen after I am gone. I have changed my life insurance policy to name each of you kids as an equal beneficiary. The policy is for $1 million, so I hope that your third will help you have a comfortable life. I regret missing so many years with you. I know this does not make up for it, but I hope you know how much I love all three of you kids. Getting to know you the past few years has been a great gift.

I am attaching the form showing this beneficiary change. You will need to contact the insurance company after my death, and I'll give you the information you will need to do that.

I'll talk to you soon.

Love,
Dad

Appendix 9-6

State of Maine
Department of Human Services
Certificate of Live Birth

Child

1a. First Name	1b. Middle Name	1c. Last Name	1d. Jr. etc.	2. Sex
Amy	Michelle	Berger		Female

3. Date of Birth (Mo. Day Yr.)	4.Time of Birth	5. County of Birth	6. City or Town of Birth
August 9, 1982	8:25 A.M.	Cumberland	Portland

7. Place of Birth:	8. Facility Name:
Hospital	Maine Medical Center

Certifier:

9. I Certify that this child was born alive at the place and time and on the date stated. *John Jacobs*	10. Date Signed (Mo. Day Yr.) August 9, 1982	11. Attendant Name (If different from Certifier)

12. Certifier's Name and Title: John J. Jacobs D.O.	13. Attendant's Mailing Address 123 Forest Ave. Portland, ME

Mother:

14. First Name	15. Middle Name		16. Last Name	17. Maiden Surname
Violet			Berger	

18. Date of Birth	19. Birthplace	20. Residence State	21. County	22. City or Town
May 1, 1960	Maine	Maine	Cumberland	Portland

23. Mother's Mailing Address		24. Zip Code	25. Years living in present town.
32 Moody St.		04101	Ten

Father:

26. First Name	27. Middle Name	28. Last Name	29. Jr., etc.
Robert		Stephenson	

30. Date of Birth	31. Birthplace
September 15, 1960	

Informant:

32. I certify that the personal information provided on this certificate is correct to the best of my knowledge and belief

Signature of Parent or other Informant: Violet Berger

———

Appendix 9-7

UNITED STATES DISTRICT COURT
EASTERN DISTRICT OF VIRGINIA

	)	
VIRGINIA LIFE INSURANCE COMPANY	)	
Plaintiff,	)	
	)	**No. 12-cv-1799829**
v.	)	
	)	
AMY BERGER,	)	
STANLEY STEPHENSON, AND	)	
STUART STEPHENSON,	)	
Defendants.	)	

STANLEY AND STUART STEPHENSON'S OBJECTIONS AND ANSWERS TO AMY BERGER'S FIRST INTERROGATORIES

Defendants Stanley and Stuart Stephenson provide the following objections and answers to Amy Berger's First Interrogatories:

***

INTERROGATORY NO. 7: Identify any documents or evidence that supports your claim that Amy Berger is not the daughter of Robert Stephenson.

ANSWER TO INTERROGATORY NO. 7: Defendants Stanley and Stuart Stephenson object that this interrogatory is premature in that discovery has just commenced. They will supplement their answer to this interrogatory when appropriate under the Federal Rules of Civil Procedure.

***

[Signed by counsel and defendants Stanley and Stuart Stephenson]

CHAPTER TEN

Post-Trial Motions
Reinvigorating Peppi's Pizza

YOU JUST COMPLETED your first jury trial, representing Peppi's Pizza in an Age Discrimination in Employment Act[1] (ADEA) case in federal court in New Mexico. Under the ADEA, it is unlawful for an employer to take an adverse action against an employee because of his age. In your case, the plaintiff Henry Joseph claimed that Peppi's fired him because of his age.

You were second chair at trial (first chair was Jessica Leslie, a partner in your firm's Labor & Employment Group). Peppi's is a regional pizza chain, with locations primarily in and around college campuses in New Mexico, Arizona, Colorado, and Utah. As second chair, you conducted the direct exam of several witnesses, covered all issues related to deposition testimony to be introduced at trial (deposition designations, objections, etc.), and handled all issues related to jury instructions.

Even though the trial was a great learning experience for you, your client lost. The jury awarded Henry $100,000 in damages.

When Henry was fired at age 49, he had worked as a Peppi's store assistant manager and later as a general manager for a combined total

---

1 *28 U.S.C.A. § 621 et seq.*

of fifteen years. At trial, Henry introduced evidence that his store was consistently one of the five (of thirty-two) most profitable Peppi's locations in his eight years as general manager. Henry had received only positive performance evaluations until his last two years with the company. At that time, Benjamin Hicks joined the company as V.P. of Operations. The jury learned that Benjamin wrote numerous e-mails and memoranda emphasizing his plan to "reinvigorate Peppi's stores." His vision included a search for "young, energetic" managers to replace "long-time managers who have grown complacent and comfortable with mediocre performance."

Benjamin instituted a system of employee feedback that included ten items that Henry's counsel characterized in closing argument as "emphasizing youth but not job performance."[2] The evidence showed that because Peppi's restaurants are located in and around college campuses, most of Peppi's servers (the people who evaluated managers) were college students. Based solely on receiving evaluations in the bottom ten percent for all Peppi's managers, Henry was placed on probation in his next to last year. When his evaluations did not improve in the next twelve months, he was fired even though his store was still one of the five most profitable stores. He was replaced by a twenty-eight year old who had been with Peppi's for only two years as a server. The evidence showed that only two other managers were terminated based on the evaluations; both were over the age of fifty and (like Henry) were replaced by managers under the age of thirty.

---

2 For example, the evaluation criteria included: "Interest in developing relationships of fun, friendship, and teamwork with employees;" "Flexibility in addressing scheduling needs of student-employees;" and "Understands the interests of college-aged customers and employees."

Peppi's witnesses maintained at trial that age was not a factor in the company's decision to fire Henry. Benjamin testified that the company was interested in attracting new customers and reinvigorating its brand and that the age of its managers was irrelevant. He explained that the employee feedback survey was designed with these goals in mind. Peppi's introduced evidence that in the twelve months following Henry's replacement, the store's profitability increased by five percent. During his cross-examination, Benjamin refused to admit that this increased profitability was related to an expansion of the store's patio dining area that occurred in the same twelve-month period and that the expansion had been suggested by Henry years earlier.

In closing argument, Jessica asked the jury to find in favor of Peppi's because Henry was fired for poor evaluations and not because of his age. Henry's counsel argued that the employee evaluation system was designed to eliminate older employees and that was exactly how it was used against Henry. To emphasize this point, he reviewed approximately ten exhibits in which Benjamin had used terms such as "youth," "young" and "reinvigorate" when describing his plan for the future of Peppi's management.

The jury found in favor of Henry on his ADEA claim. The damages award of $100,000 was consistent with plaintiff's testimony on damages and was exactly the amount plaintiff's counsel requested in closing argument. The day after the jury's verdict, the judge entered judgment in the case. Jessica Leslie has asked you to be in charge of post-trial motions.

You developed a good relationship with Rachel Brown who was Peppi's corporate representative at trial and your point person for the litigation. Rachel is not a lawyer, but she has twenty-plus years of business experience and has participated in numerous trials. She knows that you are in charge of post-trial motions, so she has written you the following e-mail.

To:	[Your name]
From:	Rachel Brown
CC:	Jessica Leslie
Subject:	Post- Trial Motions

Hi [Your name]:

Even though a couple of days have passed, I'm still shocked at the verdict in the Henry Joseph case. I do not understand how the jury could get it so wrong. Benjamin was such a good witness, and I think he did a great job explaining that this was not age discrimination. The numbers don't lie – profitability was up after Henry left the position. It's amazing to me that the jury bought Henry's story that we fired him because of his age. That's ridiculous.

Jessica told me that you are in charge of the post-trial motions. I know you are just getting started with your research, but I would appreciate a short sketch of what the motions will be, when they must be filed, what arguments we might make, and our likelihood of success. I don't need a lengthy explanation–just a page or two that could help me understand our next steps in this case. I would really appreciate getting this today if that's at all possible.

Thanks,

Rachel

You and Jessica have already met to talk through what happened at trial and the post-trial motions. The two of you agree that there were no significant legal errors at trial (evidentiary rulings, jury instructions, etc.) that could be the basis of post-trial motions. The primary argument will have to be sufficiency of the evidence to submit the case to the jury and to support the jury's verdict. You made a motion for judgment as a matter of law during trial, but that motion was denied. Based on this information and some brief research (cases in your textbook can be your primary research source unless your professor tells you to complete additional research), write an e-mail to Rachel providing answers to her questions.

 Points to Consider:

1. *ADEA Claims*. The U.S. Supreme Court has described a three-step framework for evaluating ADEA claims of intentional discrimination based on circumstantial evidence. First, the employee must establish a *prima facie* case by showing that he was over the age of forty, was qualified for the position, was discharged from that position, and was replaced by a younger employee. The burden then shifts to the employer to present evidence of a non-discriminatory reason for its decision. After the employer does so, it is then the employee's burden to show by a preponderance of the evidence that the articulated reason is a pretext for age discrimination. *Simmons v. Sykes Enterprises Inc.*, 647 F.3d 943, 947 (10th Cir. 2011), citing *McDonnell Douglas Corp. v. Green*, 93 S. Ct. 1817 (1973). To establish pretext, the employee must show that the employer's explanation "was so weak, implausible, inconsistent, or incoherent that [it] was subterfuge for discrimination." *Id.* at 947-48.

   In Henry's case, you filed a motion for summary judgment on behalf of Peppi's several months before trial. The court denied your motion, finding that "there is a genuine dispute of fact regarding whether Peppi's articulated reason for firing Henry (i.e., the evaluations) was a pretext for age discrimination." How will your argument at the post-trial stage be different from your argument at the summary judgment stage?

2. The Evidence in this Case. We learn from client representative
Rachel Brown's e-mail that the outcome of the case was a shock to her.
Apparently, she believed that the evidence favored Peppi's position
that Henry's firing was not age discrimination. As you discuss the
arguments you will make in the post-trial motions, try to see the case
from Rachel's perspective (that the evidence favored Peppi's position)
while acknowledging the challenges of prevailing on these motions.

Write an E-mail to Your Client

To: Rachel Brown

From:

CC: Jessica Leslie

Subject: Re: Post-Trial Motions

Dear Rachel,

Sincerely,

Developing Professional Skills: Civil Procedure
Local Rules, Professional Conduct Rules, and Links

Each chapter in the book is set in a specific U.S. District Court.
Listed for each chapter are the following:
- The court where the case is pending;

- A web link to the local rules for the court;

- The text of the local rule stating professional conduct standards applicable in the court;

- The text of a specific rule of professional conduct ("RPC") that your professor may choose to discuss with you when you cover the chapter; and

- A web link to the jurisdiction's rules of professional conduct.

CHAPTER ONE: PERSONAL JURISDICTION

Court: U.S. District Court, Northern District of California
Local Rules Link: http://www.cand.uscourts.gov/localrules/civil

Local Rule Stating Court's Professional Conduct Standards:
11-4. Standards of Professional Conduct
  (a) Duties and Responsibilities. Every member of the bar of this Court and any attorney permitted to practice in this Court under Civil L.R. 11 must:
  (1) Be familiar and comply with the standards of professional conduct required of members of the State Bar of California;
  (2) Comply with the Local Rules of this Court;
  (3) Maintain respect due to courts of justice and judicial officers;

(4) Practice with the honesty, care, and decorum required for the fair and efficient administration of justice;

(5) Discharge his or her obligations to his or her client and the Court; and

(6) Assist those in need of counsel when requested by the Court.

Professional Conduct Concept for this Chapter:
Pro Hac Vice Rule – Local Rule 11-3

(a) Application. An attorney who is not a member of the bar of this Court may apply to appear *pro hac vice* in a particular action in this district by filing a written application on oath certifying the following:

(1) That he or she is an active member in good standing of the bar of a United States Court or of the highest court of another State or the District of Columbia, specifying such bar;

(2) That he or she agrees to abide by the Standards of Professional Conduct set forth in Civil L.R. 11-4, and to become familiar with the Local Rules and Alternative Dispute Resolution Programs of this Court;

(3) That an attorney, identified by name, who is a member of the bar of this Court in good standing and who maintains an office within the State of California, is designated as co-counsel.

(b) Disqualification from *pro hac vice* appearance. Unless authorized by an Act of Congress or by an order of the assigned judge, an applicant is not eligible for permission to practice *pro hac vice* if the applicant:

(1) Resides in the State of California; or

(2) Is regularly engaged in the practice of law in the State of California. This disqualification shall not be applicable if the *pro hac vice* applicant (i) has been a resident of

California for less than one year; (ii) has registered with, and completed all required applications for admission to, the State Bar of California; and

(3) Has officially registered to take or is awaiting his or her results from the California State Bar exam.

(c) Approval. The Clerk shall present the application to the assigned judge for approval. The assigned judge shall have discretion to accept or reject the application.

(d) Admission Fee. Each attorney requesting to be admitted to practice under Civil L.R. 11-3 must pay to the Clerk a fee in an amount to be set by the Court. The assessment will be placed in the Court's Non-Appropriated Fund for library, educational, and other appropriate uses. If the Judge rejects the application, the attorney, upon request, shall have the fee refunded.

(e) Appearances and Service on Local Co-Counsel. All papers filed by the attorney must indicate appearance *pro hac vice*. Service of papers on and communications with local co-counsel designated pursuant to Civil L.R. 11-3(a)(3) shall constitute notice to the party.

Professional Conduct Rules Link:

http://rules.calbar.ca.gov/Rules/RulesofProfessionalConduct.aspx

CHAPTER TWO: Subject Matter Jurisdiction and Removal

Court: U.S. District Court, District of Colorado
Local Rules Link: www.cod.uscourts.gov/CourtOperations/
RulesProcedures/LocalRules/CivilLocalRules.aspx

Local Rule Stating Court's Professional Conduct Standards:
L. Civ. R. 83.4

> Except as otherwise provided by Administrative Order, the
> Colorado Rules of Professional Conduct adopted by the
> Colorado Supreme Court on April 12, 2007, and effective
> January 1, 2008, are adopted as standards of professional
> responsibility applicable in this court.

Professional Conduct Rule for this Chapter:
Colorado RPC 1.4 Communication.

> (a) A lawyer shall:
>> (1) promptly inform the client of any decision or circum-
>> stance with respect to which the client's informed consent,
>> as defined in Rule 1.0(e), is required by these Rules;
>> (2) reasonably consult with the client about the means by
>> which the client's objectives are to be accomplished;
>> (3) keep the client reasonably informed about the status of
>> the matter;
>> (4) promptly comply with reasonable requests for informa-
>> tion; and
>> (5) consult with the client about any relevant limitation on
>> the lawyer's conduct when the lawyer knows that the client
>> expects assistance not permitted by the Rules of Profes-
>> sional Conduct or other law.

> (b) A lawyer shall explain a matter to the extent reasonably nec-
> essary to permit the client to make informed decisions re-
> garding the representation.

Professional Conduct Rules Link:

http://www.cobar.org/index.cfm/ID/20472/subID/22375/CETH//

CHAPTER THREE: The Complaint

Court: U.S. District Court, District of Minnesota
Local Rules Link:

http://www.mnd.uscourts.gov/local_rules/index.shtml

Local Rule Stating Court's Professional Conduct Standards:

LR 83.6 (d): Standards for Professional Conduct.

(1) For misconduct defined in these rules, and for good cause shown, and after notice and opportunity to be heard, any attorney admitted to practice before this Court may be disbarred, suspended from practice before this Court, reprimanded or subjected to such other disciplinary action as the circumstances may warrant.

(2) Acts or omissions by an attorney admitted to practice before this Court, individually or in concert with any other person or persons, which violate the rules of professional conduct adopted by this Court shall constitute misconduct and shall be grounds for discipline, whether or not the act or omission occurred in the course of an attorney-client relationship. The Minnesota Rules of Professional Conduct adopted by the Supreme Court of Minnesota as amended from time to time by that Court are adopted by this Court except as otherwise provided by specific rules of this Court.

Professional Conduct Rule for this Chapter:

Minnesota RPC 1.6 Confidentiality of Information

(a) Except when permitted under paragraph (b), a lawyer shall not knowingly reveal information relating to the representation of a client.

(b) A lawyer may reveal information relating to the representation of a client if:

    (1) the client gives informed consent;

    (2) the information is not protected by the attorney-client privilege under applicable law, the client has not requested that the information be held inviolate, and the lawyer reasonably believes the disclosure would not be embarrassing or likely detrimental to the client;

    (3) the lawyer reasonably believes the disclosure is impliedly authorized in order to carry out the representation;

    (4) the lawyer reasonably believes the disclosure is necessary to prevent the commission of a fraud that is reasonably certain to result in substantial injury to the financial interests or property of another and in furtherance of which the client has used or is using the lawyer's services, or to prevent the commission of a crime;

    (5) the lawyer reasonably believes the disclosure is necessary to rectify the consequences of a client's criminal or fraudulent act in the furtherance of which the lawyer's services were used;

    (6) the lawyer reasonably believes the disclosure is necessary to prevent reasonably certain death or substantial bodily harm;

    (7) the lawyer reasonably believes the disclosure is necessary to secure legal advice about the lawyer's compliance with these rules;

    (8) the lawyer reasonably believes the disclosure is necessary to establish a claim or defense on behalf of the lawyer in an actual or potential controversy between the lawyer and the client, to establish a defense in a civil, criminal, or disciplinary proceeding against the lawyer based upon conduct in which the client was involved, or to respond in any proceeding to allegations by the client concerning the lawyer's representation of the client;

(9) the lawyer reasonably believes the disclosure is necessary to comply with other law or a court order; or

(10) the lawyer reasonably believes the disclosure is necessary to inform the Office of Lawyers Professional Responsibility of knowledge of another lawyer's violation of the Rules of Professional Conduct that raises a substantial question as to that lawyer's honesty, trustworthiness, or fitness as a lawyer in other respects. *See* Rule 8.3.

Professional Conduct Rules Link: http://lprb.mncourts.gov/rules/ Documents/MN Rules of Professional Conduct.pdf

CHAPTER FOUR: Motion To Dismiss For Failure To State A Claim

Court: U.S. District Court, Eastern District of Tennessee
Local Rules Link: http://www.tned.uscourts.gov/docs/localrules.htm

Local Rule Stating Court's Professional Conduct Standards:
L.R. 83.6 Rules of Professional Conduct
The Rules of Professional Conduct adopted by the Supreme Court of Tennessee are hereby adopted as rules of professional conduct insofar as they relate to matters within the jurisdiction of this Court.

Professional Conduct Rule for this Chapter:
Tennessee RPC 3.3 Candor Toward the Tribunal.
(a) A lawyer shall not knowingly:
(1) make a false statement of fact or law to a tribunal; or
(2) fail to disclose to the tribunal legal authority in the controlling jurisdiction known to the lawyer to be directly adverse to the position of the client and not disclosed by opposing counsel; or

(3) in an *ex parte* proceeding, fail to inform the tribunal of all
material facts known to the lawyer that will enable the tribunal to
make an informed decision, whether or not the facts are adverse.

Professional Conduct Rules Link:
http://www.tncourts.gov/rules/supreme-court/8

CHAPTER FIVE: The Answer

Court: U.S. District Court, Eastern District of Tennessee
Local Rules Link: http://www.tned.uscourts.gov/docs/localrules.htm

Local Rule Stating Court's Professional Conduct Standards:
L.R. 83.6 Rules of Professional Conduct
The Rules of Professional Conduct adopted by the Supreme
Court of Tennessee are hereby adopted as rules of professional
conduct insofar as they relate to matters within the jurisdiction of
this Court.

Professional Conduct Rule for this Chapter:
Tennessee RPC 5.2 Responsibilities of Subordinate Lawyer
(a) A lawyer is bound by the Rules of Professional Conduct
notwithstanding that the lawyer acted at the direction of another person.

(b) A subordinate lawyer does not violate the Rules of Professional Conduct if that lawyer acts in accordance with a super-
visory lawyer's reasonable resolution of an arguable question
of professional duty.

Professional Conduct Rules Link:
http://www.tncourts.gov/rules/supreme-court/8

CHAPTER SIX: Amending The Complaint And Relation Back

Court: U.S. District Court, Southern District of New York
Local Rules Link: http://www.nysd.uscourts.gov/rules/rules.pdf

Local Rule Stating Court's Professional Conduct Standards:
Local Civil Rule 1.5(b)(5)

In connection with activities in this Court, any attorney is found to have engaged in conduct violative of the New York State Rules of Professional Conduct as adopted from time to time by the Appellate Divisions of the State of New York. In interpreting the Code, in the absence of binding authority from the United States Supreme Court or the United States Court of Appeals for the Second Circuit, this Court, in the interests of comity and predictability, will give due regard to decisions of the New York Court of Appeals and other New York State courts, absent significant federal interests.

Professional Conduct Rules for this Chapter:
New York RPC 1.2. Scope of Representation and Allocation of Authority Between Client and Lawyer

(a) Subject to the provisions herein, a lawyer shall abide by a client's decisions concerning the objectives of representation and, as required by Rule 1.4, shall consult with the client as to the means by which they are to be pursued. A lawyer shall abide by a client's decision whether to settle a matter. In a criminal case, the lawyer shall abide by the client's decision, after consultation with the lawyer, as to a plea to be entered, whether to waive jury trial and whether the client will testify.

New York RPC 1.4(a)(2) Communication

A lawyer shall reasonably consult with the client about the means by which the client's objectives are to be accomplished.

Professional Conduct Rules Link:

http://www.nysba.org/Content/NavigationMenu/ForAttorneys/Professional Standards for Attorneys/NYRulesofProfessionalConduct4109.pdf

CHAPTER SEVEN: Disclosure And Discovery Tools And Planning

Court: U.S. District Court, Northern District of California
Local Rules Link: http://www.cand.uscourts.gov/localrules/civil

Local Rule Stating Court's Professional Conduct Standards:
11-4. Standards of Professional Conduct

   (a) Duties and Responsibilities. Every member of the bar of this Court and any attorney permitted to practice in this Court under Civil L.R. 11 must:

      (1) Be familiar and comply with the standards of professional conduct required of members of the State Bar of California;

      (2) Comply with the Local Rules of this Court;

      (3) Maintain respect due to courts of justice and judicial officers;

      (4) Practice with the honesty, care, and decorum required for the fair and efficient administration of justice;

      (5) Discharge his or her obligations to his or her client and the Court; and

      (6) Assist those in need of counsel when requested by the Court.

Professional Conduct Rule for this Chapter:
California RPC 5-220 Suppression of Evidence

   A member shall not suppress any evidence that the member or the member's client has a legal obligation to reveal or to produce.

Professional Conduct Rules Link:

http://rules.calbar.ca.gov/LinkClick.aspx?fileticket=8qtNkWP-Kjw%3D&tabid=476

CHAPTER EIGHT: Inadvertent Disclosure

Court: U.S. District Court, Middle District of Florida
Local Rules Link: http://www.flmd.uscourts.gov/Forms/USDC-MDFL-LocalRules12-2009.pdf

Local Rule Stating Court's Professional Conduct Standards:
Local Rule 2.04

> (d) The professional conduct of all members of the bar of this Court, admitted generally under Rule 2.01 or specially under Rule 2.02, shall be governed by the Model Rules of Professional Conduct of the American Bar Association as modified and adopted by the Supreme Court of Florida to govern the professional behavior of the members of The Florida Bar.

Professional Conduct Rule for this Chapter:
Florida RPC 4.4 Respect for Rights of Third Persons

> (b) A lawyer who receives a document relating to the representation of the lawyer's client and knows or reasonably should know that the document was inadvertently sent shall promptly notify the sender.

Professional Conduct Rules Link: https://www.floridabar.org/divexe/rrtfb.nsf/FV/A31CADC44C510AD7852571710072AB8A

CHAPTER NINE: Summary Judgment

Court: U.S. District Court, Eastern District of Virginia

Local Rules Link: http://www.vaed.uscourts.gov/localrules/Local-RulesEDVA.pdf

Local Rules Stating Court's Professional Conduct Standards:

Local Civil Rule 83.1(I) Professional Ethics:

> The ethical standards relating to the practice of law in civil cases in this Court shall be Section II of Part Six of the Rules of the Virginia Supreme Court as it may be amended or superceded from time to time.

Appendix B – Federal Rules of Disciplinary Enforcement—
FRDE RULE IV (B)

> Acts or omissions by an attorney admitted to practice before this Court, individually or in concert with any other person or persons, which violate the Virginia Rules of Professional Conduct adopted by this Court shall constitute misconduct and shall be grounds for discipline, whether or not the act or omission occurred in the course of any attorney-client relationship.
> The Rules of Professional Conduct adopted by this Court are the Rules of Professional Conduct adopted by the highest Court of the state in which this Court sits, as amended from time to time by that state Court, except as otherwise provided by specific Rule of this Court after consideration of comments by representatives of bar associations within the state.

Professional Conduct Rule for this Chapter:

Virginia RPC Rule 4.2: Communication With
Persons Represented By Counsel

> In representing a client, a lawyer shall not communicate about the subject of the representation with a person the lawyer knows to be represented by another lawyer in the matter, unless the